UKULELE

TOP HITS OF 2019

20 HOT SINGLES

ISBN 978-1-5400-6462-2

Motion Picture Artwork TM & Copyright © 2019 Disney

Visit Hal Leonard Online at
www.halleonard.com

Contact us:
Hal Leonard
7777 West Bluemound Road
Milwaukee, WI 53213
Email: info@halleonard.com

In Europe, contact:
Hal Leonard Europe Limited
42 Wigmore Street
Marylebone, London, W1U 2RN
Email: info@halleonardeurope.com

In Australia, contact:
Hal Leonard Australia Pty. Ltd.
4 Lentara Court
Cheltenham, Victoria, 3192 Australia
Email: info@halleonard.com.au

CONTENTS

Bad Guy

Words and Music by Billie Eilish O'Connell and Finneas O'Connell

First note

Verse
Moderately fast

1. White shirt now red: ___ my blood - y nose.
3. I like it when ___ you take ___ con - trol.

Sleep - ing. You're on ___ your tip - py toes, creep - ing a - round ___
E - ven if you ___ know that ___ you don't own me, I'll let ___

___ like no ___ one knows. Think you're so crim - i - nal.
___ you play ___ the role: I'll be your crim - i - nal.

Verse

2. Bruis - es on both ___ my knees ___ for you. Don't say thank you ___
4. My mom - my likes ___ to sing ___ a - long with me, but she ___

* Lead vocal written an octave higher than sung.

_____ or please. _____ I do what I want, when _____ I'm want - ing to.
_____ won't sing _____ this song. If she reads all _____ the lyr - ics, she'll

My soul, so cyn - i - cal.
pit - y the men _____ I know.

Chorus

tough guy, "I like it real - ly rough" guy, "I just can't get e -

nough" guy, "chest al - ways so puffed" guy. I'm that

bad type, "make your ma - ma sad" type, "make your girl - friend

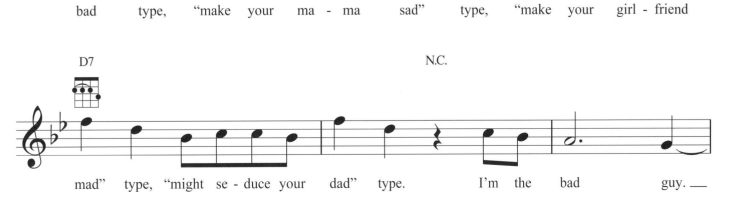

mad" type, "might se - duce your dad" type. I'm the bad guy. _____

Interlude

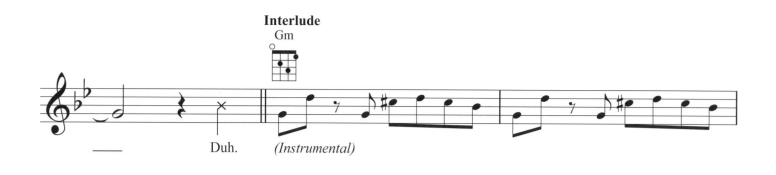

Duh. *(Instrumental)*

I'm the bad guy. —

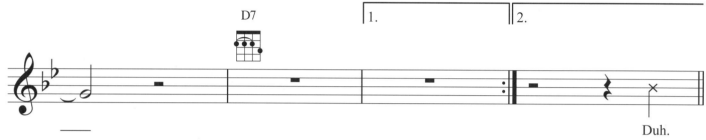

— Duh.

Outro

(Instrumental)

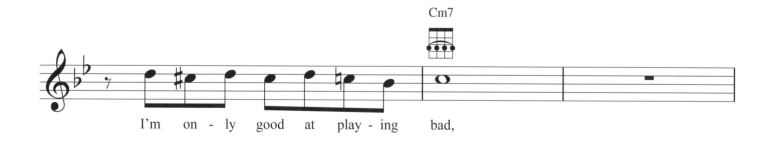

I'm on-ly good at play-ing bad,

bad.

Close to Me

**Words and Music by Anders Svensson, Savan Kotecha,
Thomas Pentz, Elena Goulding, Ilya and Khalif Brown**

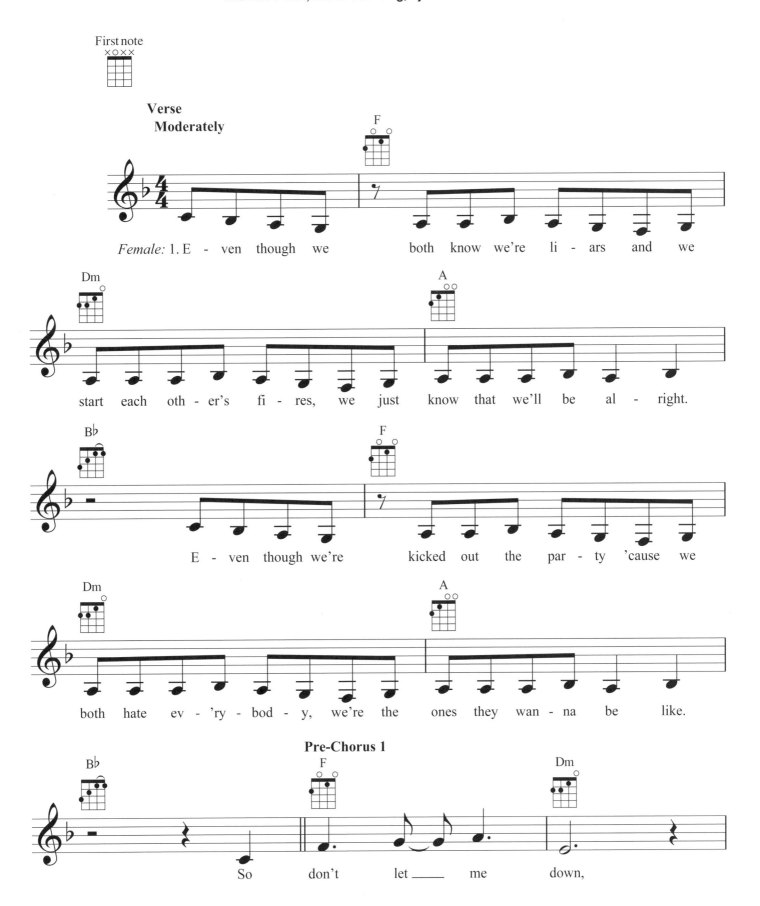

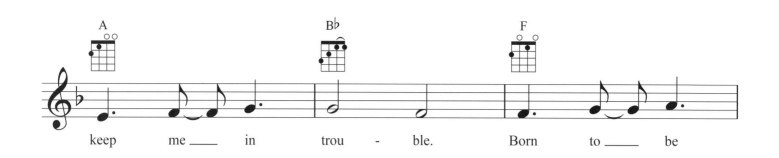

keep me _____ in trou - ble. Born to _____ be

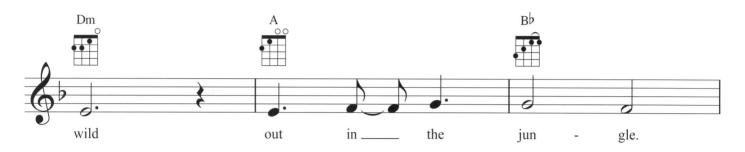

wild out in _____ the jun - gle.

Chorus

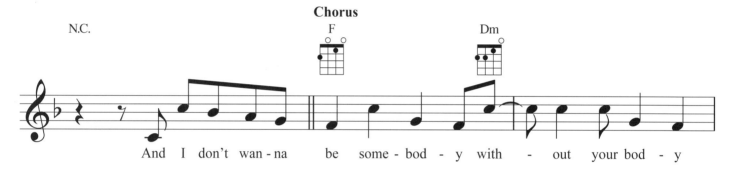

And I don't wan - na be some - bod - y with - out your bod - y

close to me. _____ And if it was - n't you, I would - n't want _____

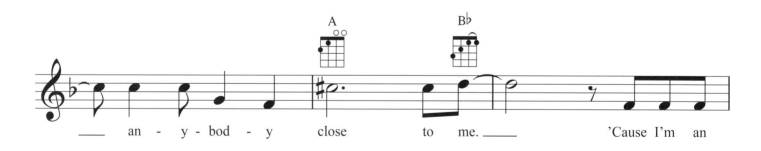

_____ an - y - bod - y close to me. _____ 'Cause I'm an

an - i - mal, an - i - mal _____ like, an - i - mal _____ like _____

Price tag pop - pin', then ___ you wan - na bribe me. Don't say sor - ry, ev -

- 'ry-one's watch - in'. When you where I am, ev - 'ry-thing's time - less.

§ **Chorus**

N.C.

Female: And I don't wan - na be some - bod - y with - out your bod - y

close to me. ___ And if it was - n't you, I would - n't want __

___ an - y - bod - y close to me. ___ 'Cause I'm an

an - i - mal, an - i - mal ___ like, an - i - mal, ___ like ___

you. And I don't wan - na be some - bod - y with - out your bod - y

close to me, ____ close to me. ____ *(Vocal 1st time only)*

An - i - mal, an - i -

mal ____ like, an - i - mal ____ like ____ you. And I don't wan - na

Outro

____ *(Vocal 1st time only)*

Break Up with Your Girlfriend, I'm Bored

Words and Music by Ariana Grande, Kandi Burruss, Kevin Briggs, Savan Kotecha, Max Martin and Ilya

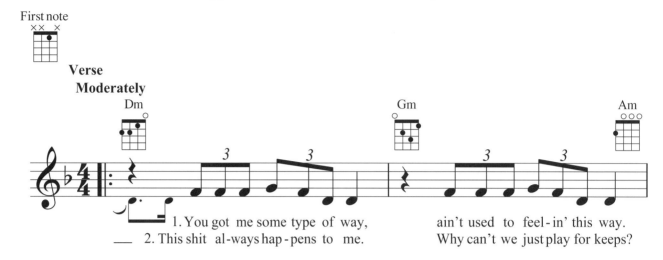

1. You got me some type of way, ain't used to feel-in' this way.
2. This shit al-ways hap-pens to me. Why can't we just play for keeps?

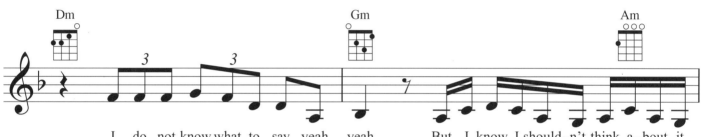

I do not know what to say, yeah, yeah. But I know I should-n't think a-bout it.
Prac-ti-cal-ly on my knees, yeah, yeah. But I know I should-n't think a-bout it.

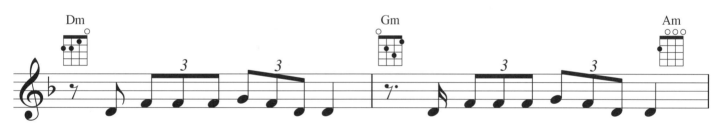

Took one fuck-in' look at your face, now I wan-na know how you taste.
You know what you're do-in' to me. You're sing-in' my songs in the streets, yeah

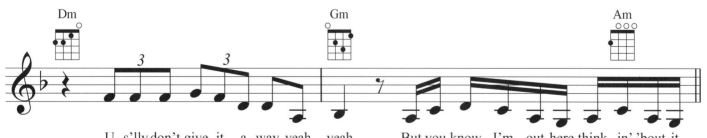

U-s'lly don't give it a-way, yeah, yeah. But you know I'm out here think-in' 'bout it.
yeah. Act-in' all in-no-cent, please, _____ when I know you're out here think-in' 'bout it.

Gloria

Words and Music by Jeremy Fraites and Wesley Schultz

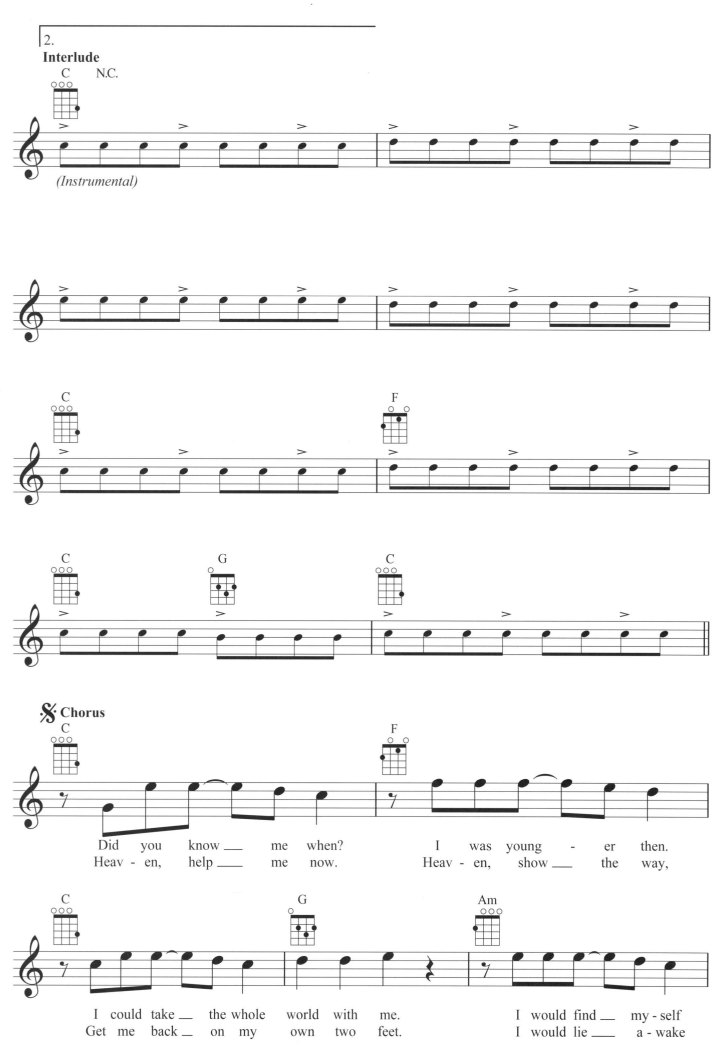

Oh, _____ oh, _____ oh, _____ _____ oh, _____ oh. _____

3. Glo - ri - a,
4. Glo - ri - a,

you crawled _ up on _____ your cross. _____
will _____ you just _____ de - cide? _____

Glo - ri - a, you made _____ us sit _____ and watch. _
Glo - ri - a, there's eas - ier ways _ to die. _____

_____ Glo - ri - a, _____ no _____
_____ Glo - ri - a, _____ have _____

_____ one said _____ e - nough _____ is _____ e - nough.
_____ you had _____ e - nough? _____

To Coda

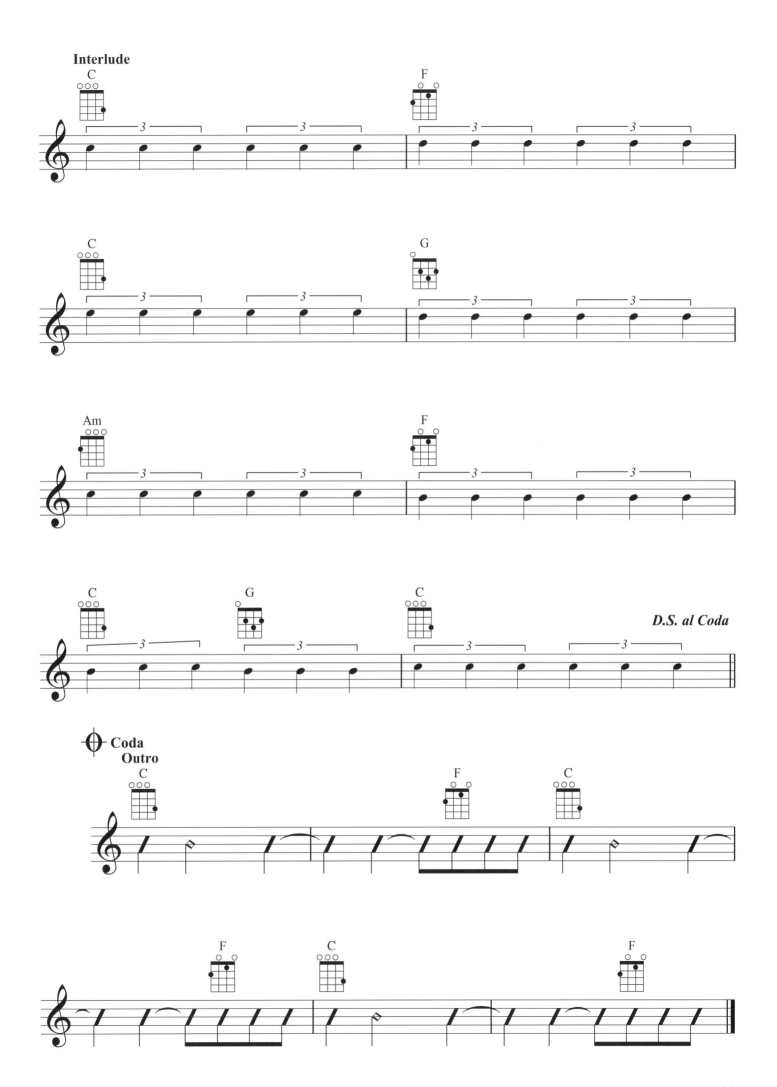

Dancing with a Stranger

Words and Music by Sam Smith, Tor Hermansen,
Mikkel Eriksen, Normani Hamilton and James Napier

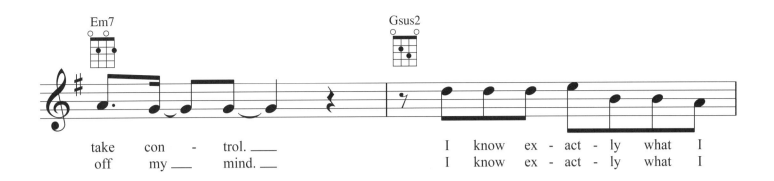

take con - trol. ____ I know ex - act - ly what I
off my ___ mind. __ I know ex - act - ly what I

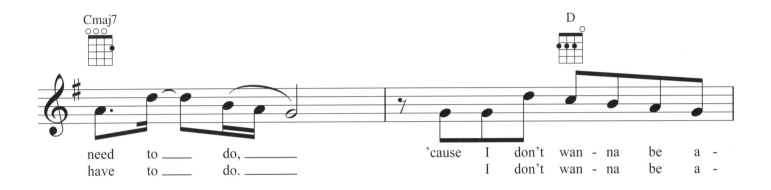

need to ___ do, _____ 'cause I don't wan - na be a -
have to ___ do. ___ I don't wan - na be a -

lone to - night, a - lone to - night, a - lone to - night. _
lone to - night, a - lone to - night, a - lone to - night. _

Chorus

Look what you made me do; I'm with some - bod - y new. Ooh, ba - by, ba - by, I'm danc -

- ing with a stran - ger. Look what you made me do; I'm with some - bod - y new.

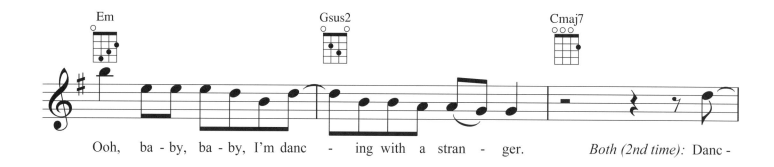

Ooh, ba - by, ba - by, I'm danc - ing with a stran - ger. *Both (2nd time):* Danc -

1.

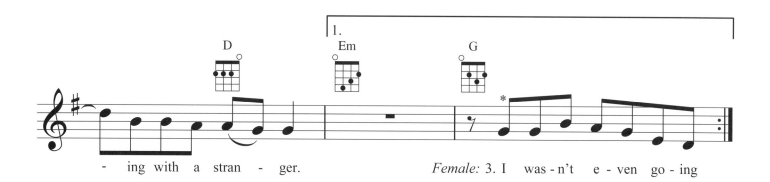

- ing with a stran - ger. *Female:* 3. I was - n't e - ven go - ing

2.

Danc - ing with a stran - ger. *Male:* Danc -

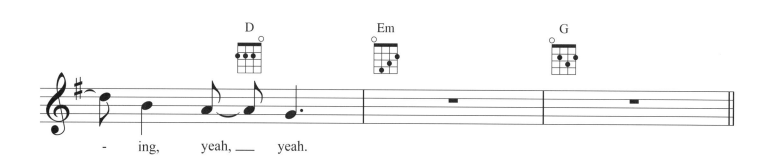

- ing, yeah, ___ yeah.

Chorus

Look what you made me do; I'm with some - bod - y new. Ooh, ba - by, ba - by, I'm danc -

* *Female vocal sung one octave lower.*

- ing with a stran - ger. *Both:* Look what you made me do; I'm with some-bod-y new.

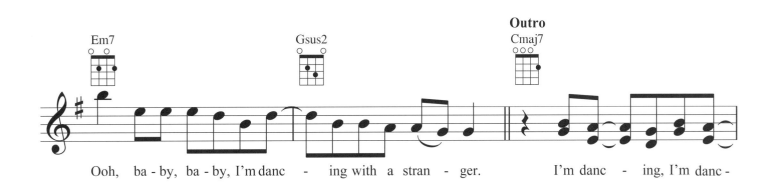

Outro

Ooh, ba - by, ba - by, I'm danc - ing with a stran - ger. I'm danc - ing, I'm danc -

- ing. (I'm danc - ing, I'm danc - ing.) *Male:* Danc - ing with a stran - ger. ____

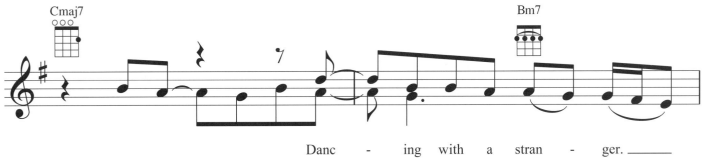

Female: I'm danc - ing, I'm danc - ing. Danc - ing with a stran - ger. _____

(I'm danc - ing, I'm danc - ing.) *Female:* Danc - ing with a stran - ger.

I Don't Care

Words and Music by Ed Sheeran, Justin Bieber, Fred Gibson, Jason Boyd, Max Martin and Shellback

Ev-'ry-one's got so much to   say,   yeah. __   I   al - ways feel like I'm no-
Ev-'ry-one's got so much to   say, oh yeah. _____   When we walked in,   I said, "I'm

bod - y,   mm. __   Who wants to   fit in   an - y - way? }
sor - ry,"   mm. __   But now I think that we should   stay. }   'Cause I don't

Chorus

care   when I'm with my ba - by, yeah. __   All   the bad things dis - ap - pear. __

And you're mak - ing me feel like   may - be I am some - bod - y. __

I can deal   with the bad   nights _____   when I'm with my ba - by, yeah. __

Ooh ooh ooh ooh   ooh ___   ooh. __   'Cause I don't

care as long as you just hold me near. ___ You can take me an-y-where. __

Em

___ And you're mak-ing me feel like I'm loved by some-bod-y. ___

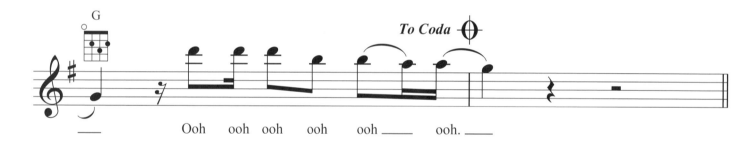

C   **D**

I can deal with the bad nights _____ when I'm with my ba-by, yeah. _

G   *To Coda* ⊕

___ Ooh ooh ooh ooh ooh ___ ooh. ___

Verse
N.C.

G

2. We at a par-ty we don't wan-na be at,   tryin' to talk, but we can't hear __ our-

Em

selves. __ Read your lips, I'd rath-er kiss 'em right back. _ With all these peo-ple all a-round _ I'm crip-

26

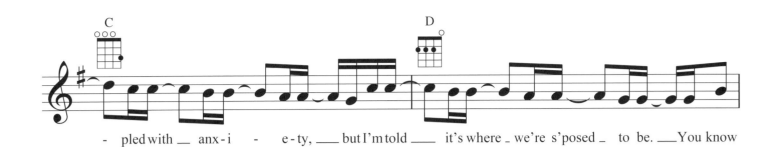

- pled with __ anx - i - e - ty, ___ but I'm told ___ it's where _ we're s'posed _ to be. ___You know

D.S. al Coda

what? It's kind of cra - zy 'cause I real - ly don't mind ___ when _ you make it bet-ter like that.

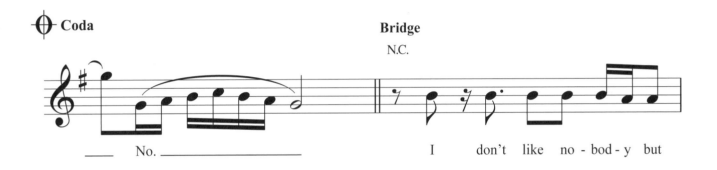

Coda

Bridge

N.C.

___ No. _____ I don't like no - bod - y but

you. It's like you're the on - ly one here. I don't like no - bod - y but

you, ba - by. I don't care. I don't like no - bod - y but

you. I hate ev - 'ry - one here. I don't like no - bod - y but

If I Can't Have You

Words and Music by Shawn Mendes, Teddy Geiger,
Nate Mercereau and Scott Harris

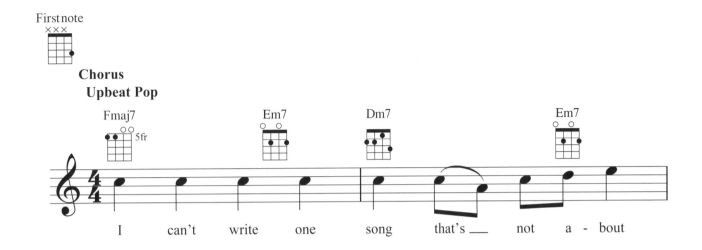

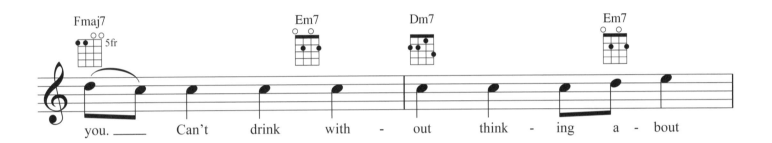

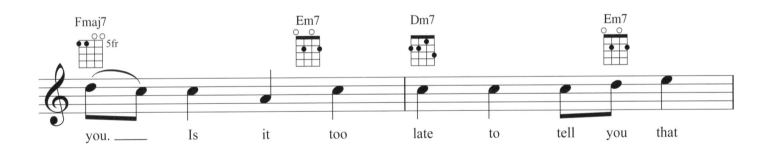

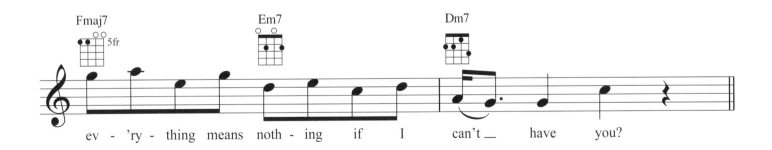

Bridge

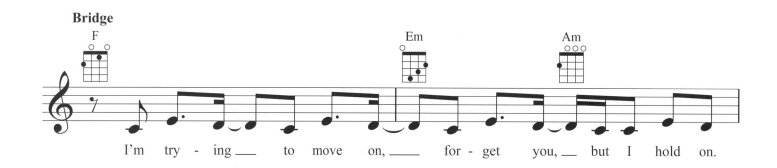

I'm try - ing ___ to move on, ___ for - get you, ___ but I hold on.

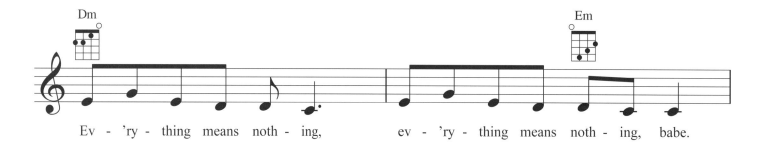

Ev - 'ry - thing means noth - ing, ev - 'ry - thing means noth - ing, babe.

I'm try - ing ___ to move on, ___ for - get you, ___ but I hold on.

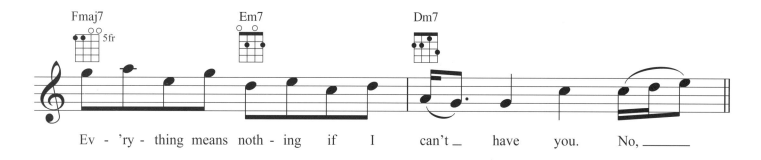

Ev - 'ry - thing means noth - ing if I can't ___ have you. No, ___

Chorus

N.C.

I can't write one song that's ___ not a - bout

you. ___ Can't drink with - out think - ing a - bout

you. _____ Is it too late to tell you that

ev - 'ry - thing means noth - ing if I can't _ have you?

Chorus

Fmaj7   Em7   Dm7   Em7

I can't write one song that's _____ not a - bout

Fmaj7   Em7   Dm7   Em7

you. _____ Can't drink with - out think - ing a - bout

Fmaj7   Em7   Dm7   Em7

you. _____ Is it too late to tell you that

Fmaj7   Em7   Dm7

ev - 'ry - thing means noth - ing if I can't _ have you?

Lo/Hi

Words and Music by Dan Auerbach and Patrick Carney

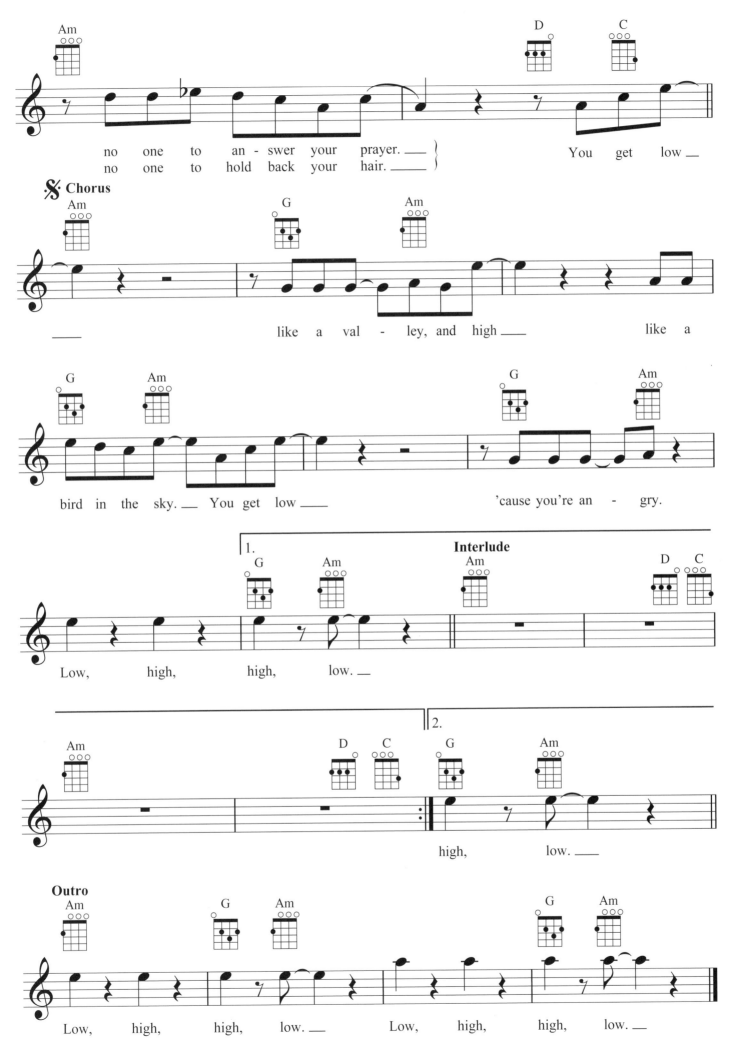

ME!

Words and Music by Taylor Swift, Joel Little and Brendon Urie

Intro
Moderately, in 2

Female: I prom - ise that you'll nev - er find an - oth - er like me.

Verse

1. I know that I'm a hand - ful, ba - by, uh. I know I nev - er

think be - fore I jump. And you're the kind of guy the la - dies

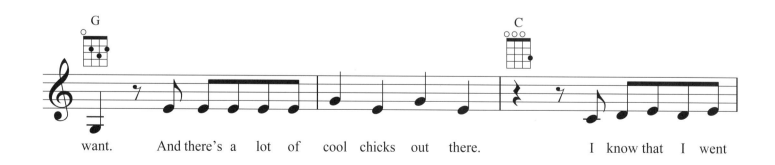

want. And there's a lot of cool chicks out there. I know that I went

psy - cho on the phone. I nev - er leave _ well e - nough a -

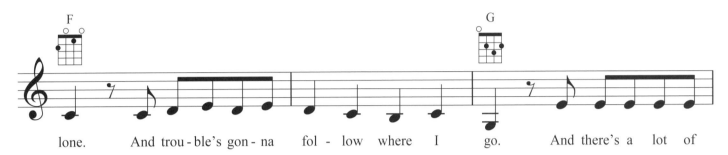

lone. And trou - ble's gon - na fol - low where I go. And there's a lot of

Pre-Chorus

N.C.

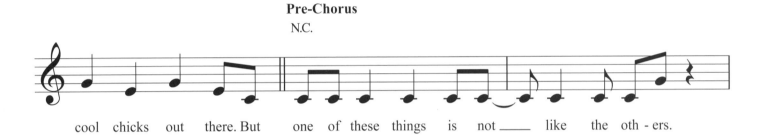

cool chicks out there. But one of these things is not ___ like the oth - ers.

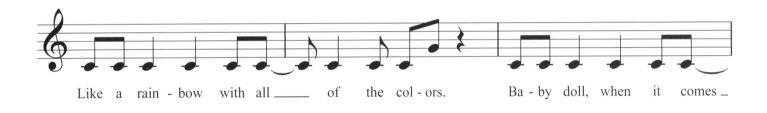

Like a rain - bow with all ___ of the col - ors. Ba - by doll, when it comes _

___ to a lov - er, I prom - ise that you'll nev - er find an - oth - er like me, ee

Chorus

ee.   Ooh, ooh, ooh. _____

I'm the on - ly one of me. _____ Ba - by, that's the fun of me,

ee ee ee. _____ Ooh, ooh, ooh. _____

_____ You're the on - ly one of you. _____

Ba - by, that's the fun of you. _____ And I prom - ise that no - bod - y's gon - na

Verse

love you like me, ee ee. *Male:* 2. I know I tend to make it a - bout

me. I know you nev - er get just what you see. But I will nev - er

bore   you,   ba -   by.   And there's   a   lot   of   lame   guys   out   there.

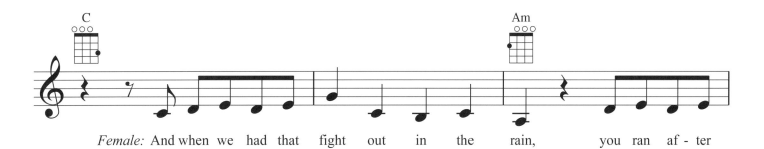

Female: And when   we   had   that   fight   out   in   the   rain,   you   ran   af - ter

me   and   called   my   name.   *Male:* I   nev - er   wan - na   see   you   walk   a -

Pre-Chorus
N.C.

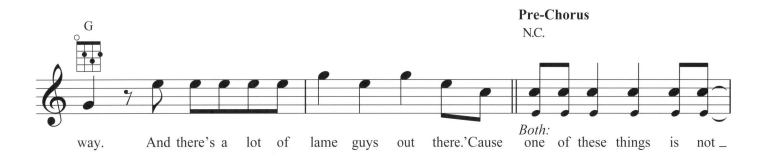

Both:

way.   And there's   a   lot   of   lame   guys   out   there. 'Cause   one   of   these   things   is   not __

___ like   the   oth - ers.   Liv - ing   in   win - ter,   I _____   am   your   sum - mer.

Ba - by   doll,   when   it   comes __   to   a   lov - er,   *Male:* I   prom - ise   that   you'll   nev - er   find   an -

Bridge

spell - ing is fun! Girl, there ain't no I _____ in team,

but you know there is _____ a me. Strike the band up, one, _

_____ two, three. *Female:* I prom-ise that you'll nev - er find an - oth - er like me.

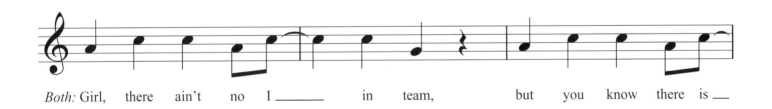

Both: Girl, there ain't no I _____ in team, but you know there is _

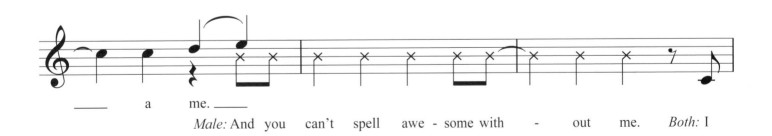

_____ a me. _____
Male: And you can't spell awe - some with - out me. *Both:* I

D.S. al Coda

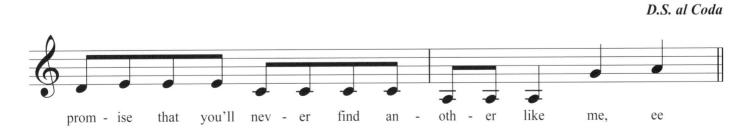

prom - ise that you'll nev - er find an - oth - er like me, ee

Coda
Outro-Chorus

ee.

Girl, there ain't no I _____ in team, but you know there is _____ a me. ___

I'm the on - ly one of me. _____ Ba - by, that's the fun of me,

ee ee ee. Strike the band up, one, _____ two, three. You

can't spell awe - some with - out me. _____ You're the on - ly one of you. ___

_____ Ba - by, that's the fun of you. _____ And I

prom - ise that no - bod - y's gon - na love you like me, ee ee.

Never Really Over

Words and Music by Katy Perry, Michelle Buzz, Jason Gill, Gino Barletta, Hayley Warner,
Dagny Sandvik, Anton Zaslavski, Leah Haywood and Daniel James Pringle

1. I'm los - ing my self - con - trol.

Yeah, you're start - ing to trick - le back in. ___

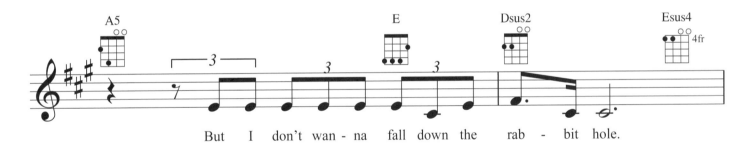

But I don't wan - na fall down the rab - bit hole.

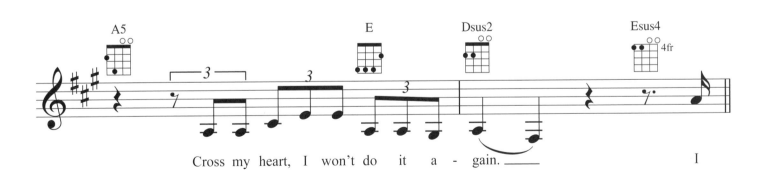

Cross my heart, I won't do it a - gain. ___   I

guess it's nev-er real-ly o - ver. _____ Thought _ we drew the _ line

right _ through you and _ I.   Can't _ keep go-ing back; _ I

guess it's nev - er real-ly o - ver. _____

Pre-Chorus 2

Two years and just like _ that,   my head still takes me _ back.

Thought it was done, but _ I guess it's nev-er real-ly o - ver. Just _

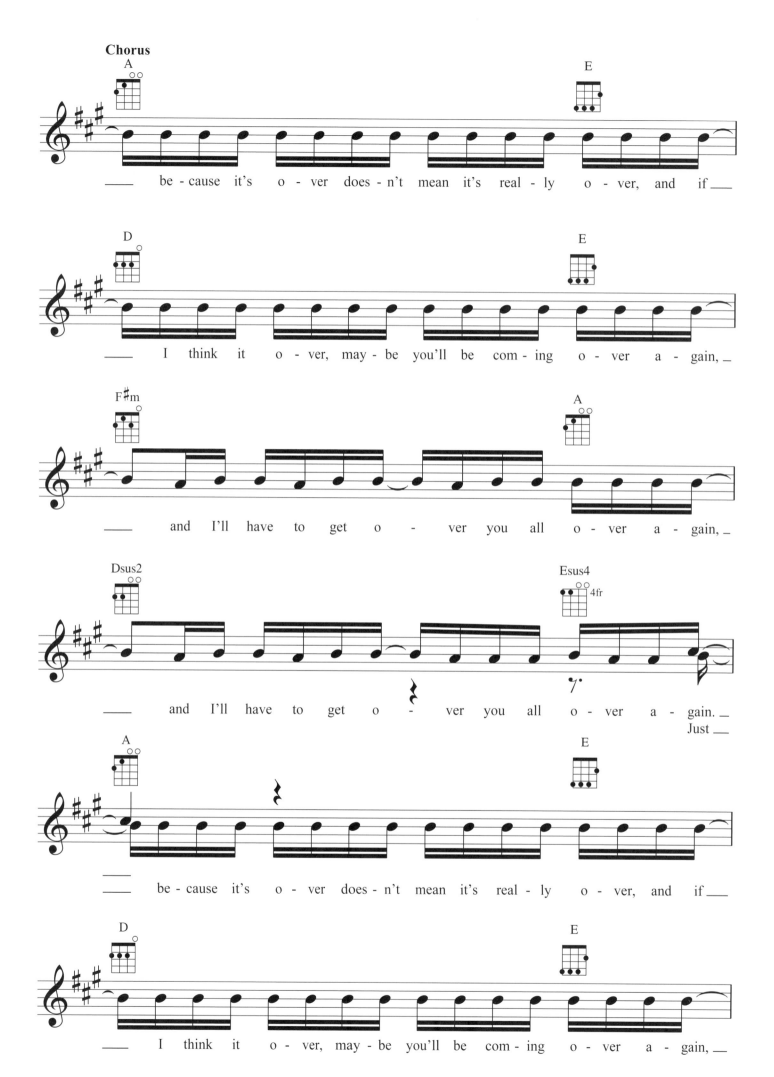

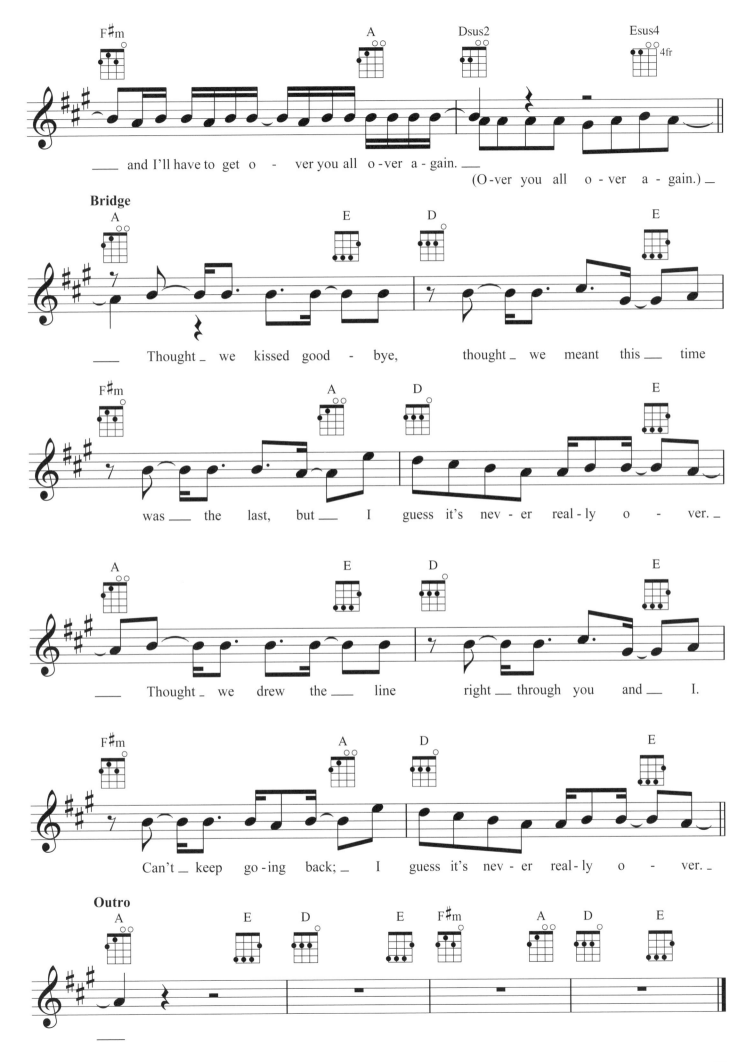

Old Town Road

(Remix)

Words and Music by Trent Reznor, Billy Ray Cyrus, Jocelyn Donald,
Atticus Ross, Kiowa Roukema and Montero Lamar Hill

Ma - se - ra - ti sports car. Got no stress; I've been through all that. I'm like a

Marl - boro Man, so I kick on back. Wish I could roll on back to that old

town road. I wan - na ride till I can't no more. Yeah, I'm gon - na

Chorus

take my horse to the old town road. I'm gon-na ride till I can't no more. I'm gon-na

take my horse to the old town road. I'm gon-na ride till I can't no more.

Outro

Repeat and fade

(Instrumental)

7 Rings

Words and Music by Richard Rodgers, Oscar Hammerstein II, Ariana Grande, Victoria McCants,
Kimberly Krysiuk, Tayla Parx, Tommy Brown, Njomza Vitia, Michael Foster and Charles Anderson

1. Break-fast at Tif-f'ny's and bot-tles of bub-bles. Girls with tat-toos who like
2. Wear-ing a ring, but ain't gon' be no Mis-sus. Bought match-ing dia-monds for

get-ting in trou-ble. Lash-es and dia-monds, A - T - M ma-chines.
six of my bitch-es. I'd rath-er spoil all my friends with my rich-es.

Buy my-self all of my fa-vor-ite things. Been through some bad shit; I
Think re-tail ther-a-py's my new ad-dic-tion. Who-ev-er said mon-ey

should be a sad bitch. Who would have thought it'd turn me to a sav-age?
can't solve your prob-lems must not have had e-nough mon-ey to solve them.

Rath - er be tied up with cuffs and not strings.
They say, "Which one?" I say, "Nah, I want all them."

Write my own checks like I
Hap - pi - ness is the same

Pre-Chorus

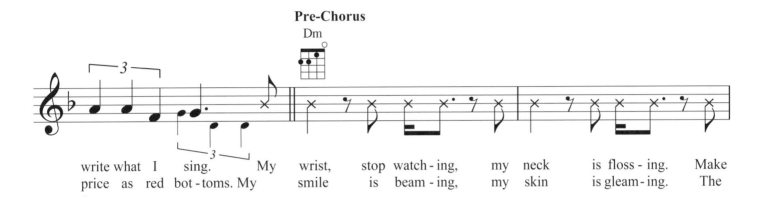

write what I sing. My wrist, stop watch - ing, my neck is floss - ing. Make
price as red bot - toms. My smile is beam - ing, my skin is gleam - ing. The

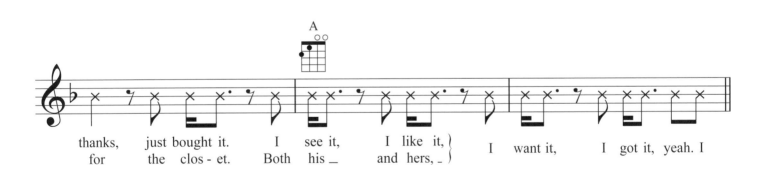

big de - pos - its, my gloss is pop - ping. You like my hair? Gee,
way it shine, _ I know you've seen it. I bought a crib just

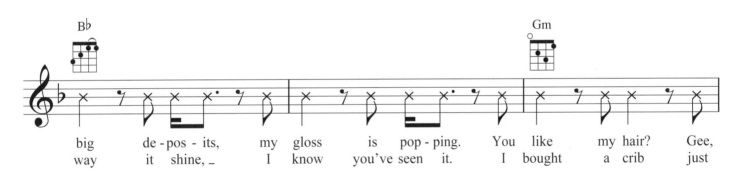

thanks, just bought it. I see it, I like it,
for the clos - et. Both his _ and hers, _

I want it, I got it, yeah. I

𝄋 Chorus

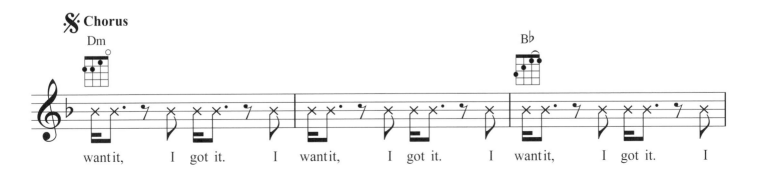

want it, I got it. I want it, I got it. I want it, I got it. I

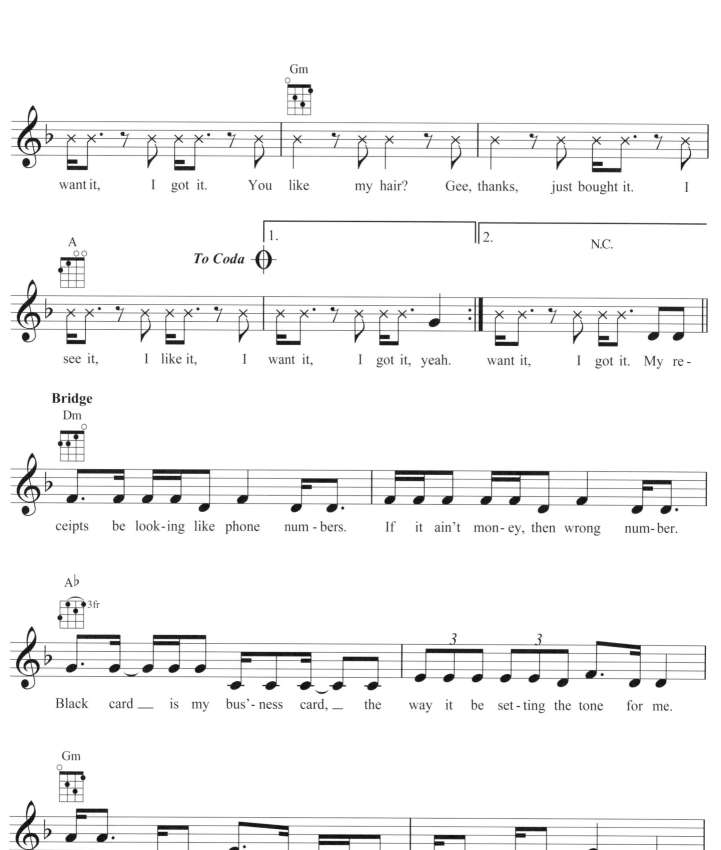

Gm

want it,   I got it.   You like   my hair?   Gee, thanks,   just bought it.   I

A

1.

To Coda ⊕

2.   N.C.

see it,   I like it,   I want it,   I got it, yeah.   want it,   I got it. My re-

Bridge

Dm

ceipts be look-ing like phone num-bers.   If it ain't mon-ey, then wrong num-ber.

A♭ 3fr

3   3

Black card __ is my bus'-ness card, __ the way it be set-ting the tone for me.

Gm

I don't mean to brag, but I be like, "Put it in the bag," yeah.

A

When you see them racks, they stacked up like my ass, ___ yeah.

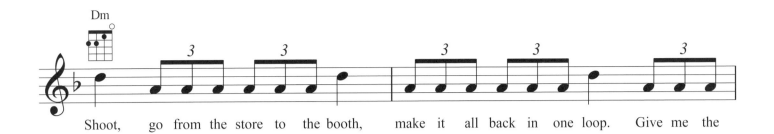

Shoot, go from the store to the booth, make it all back in one loop. Give me the

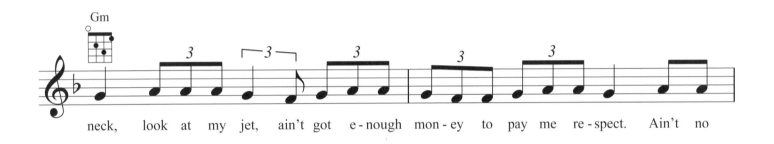

loot; nev-er mind, I got the juice. Noth-ing but net when we shoot. Look at my

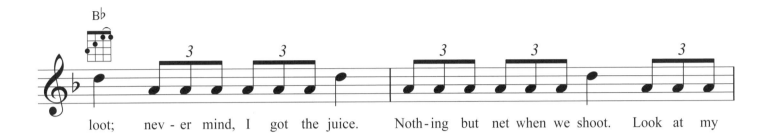

neck, look at my jet, ain't got e-nough mon-ey to pay me re-spect. Ain't no

D.S. al Coda

bud-get when I'm on the set. If I like it, then that's what I get, yeah. I

Outro

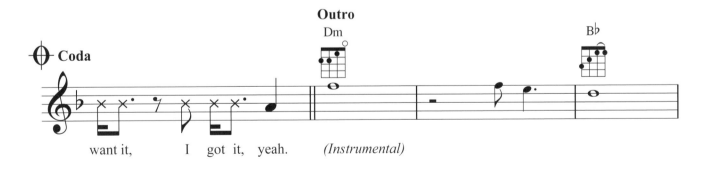

want it, I got it, yeah. *(Instrumental)*

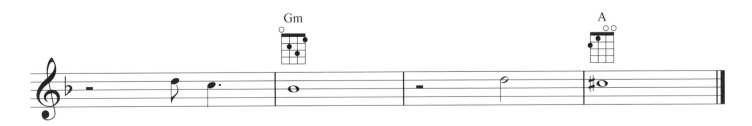

Someone You Loved

**Words and Music by Lewis Capaldi, Benjamin Kohn,
Peter Kelleher, Thomas Barnes and Samuel Roman**

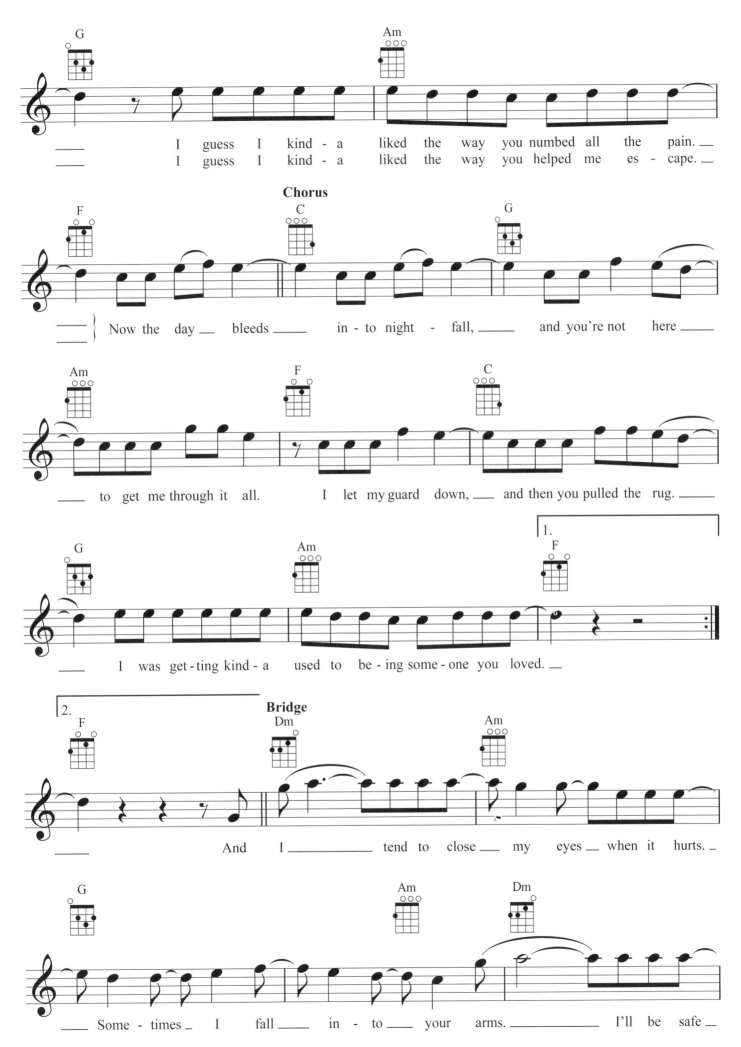

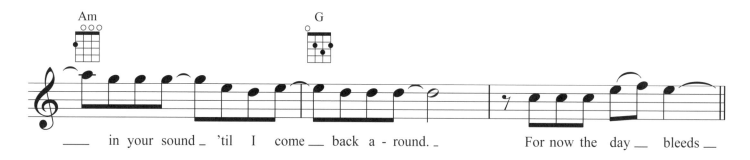

_____ in your sound _ 'til I come _ back a - round. _ For now the day _ bleeds _

Chorus

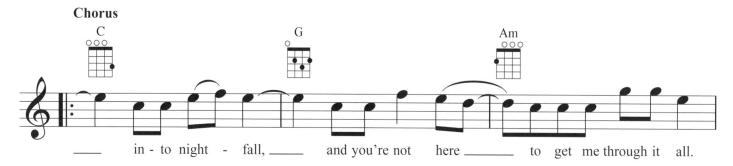

_____ in - to night - fall, _____ and you're not here _____ to get me through it all.

I let my guard down, ___ and then you pulled the rug. _____ I was get - ting kind - a

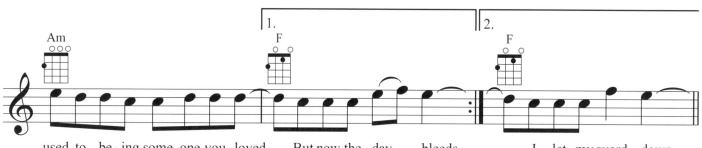

1. 2.

used to be - ing some-one you loved. _ But now the day _ bleeds _ _ I let my guard down, _

Outro

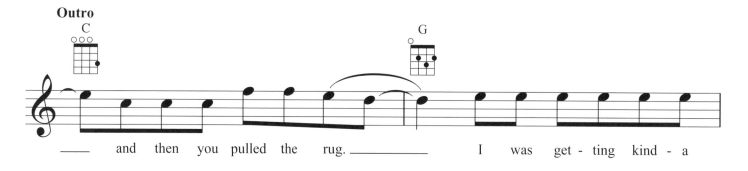

_____ and then you pulled the rug. _____ I was get - ting kind - a

slight rit.

used to be - ing some-one you loved. _

Señorita

Words and Music by Camila Cabello, Charlotte Aitchison, Jack Patterson, Shawn Mendes, Magnus Høiberg, Benjamin Levin, Ali Tamposi and Andrew Wotman

%: **Chorus**

call me "se-ño-ri-ta." I wish I could pre-tend I did-n't need __

__ ya, but ev-'ry touch is ooh, la, __ la, la. It's true, la, __ la, la. Ooh, __

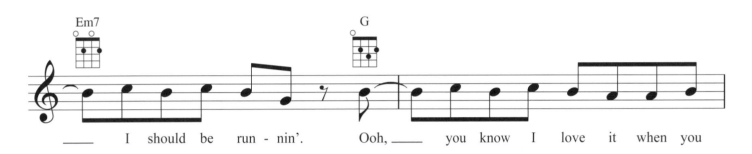

__ I should be run-nin'. Ooh, __ you know I love it when you

call me "se-ño-ri-ta." I wish it was-n't so damn hard to leave __

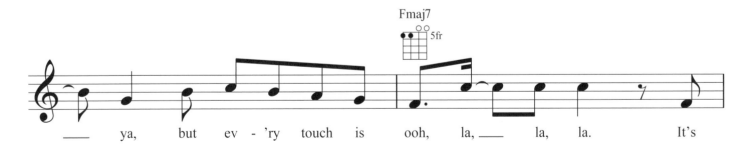

__ ya, but ev-'ry touch is ooh, la, __ la, la. It's

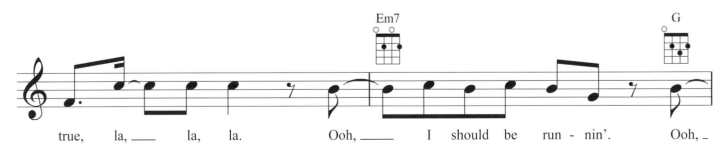

true, la, __ la, la. Ooh, __ I should be run-nin'. Ooh, __

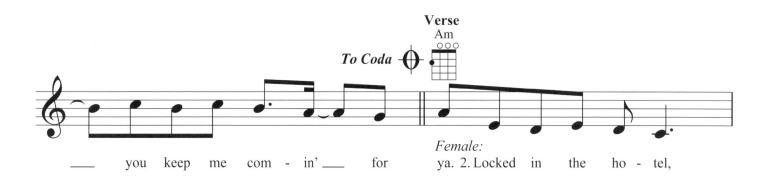

Verse

you keep me com - in' ___ for ya. 2. Locked in the ho - tel,

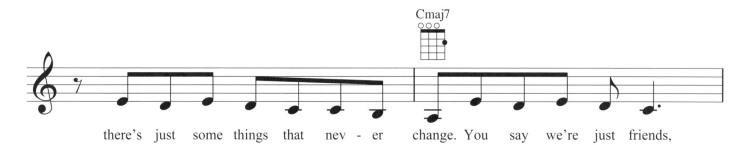

there's just some things that nev - er change. You say we're just friends,

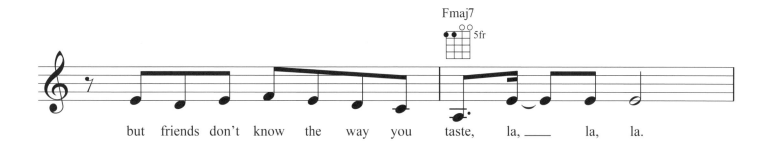

but friends don't know the way you taste, la, ___ la, la.

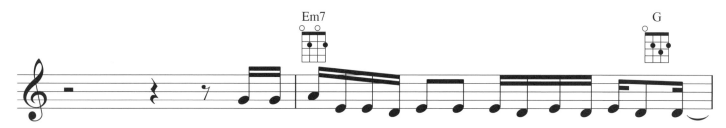

'Cause you know it's been a long time com - in', don't you let me fall, ___

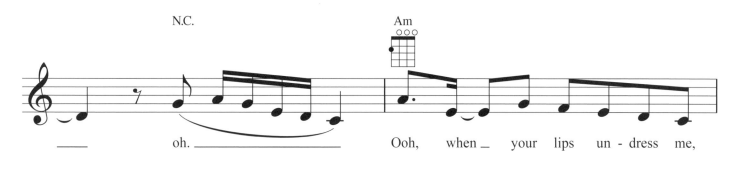

___ oh. ___ Ooh, when ___ your lips un - dress me,

hooked on ___ your tongue. Ooh, love, ___ your kiss is dead - ly. Don't stop. I love it when you

64

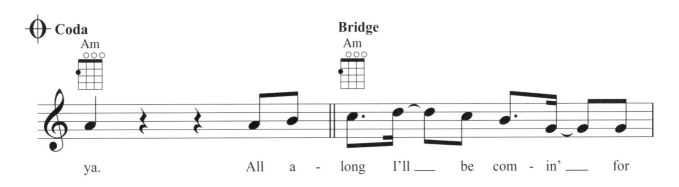

Coda

Bridge

ya.   All a - long I'll ___ be com - in' ___ for

ya.   And I hope it ___ meant some - thin' ___ to ya.   Call my

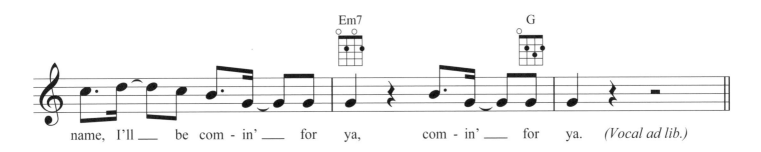

name, I'll ___ be com - in' ___ for ya,   com - in' ___ for ya.   *(Vocal ad lib.)*

Outro

(Instrumental)

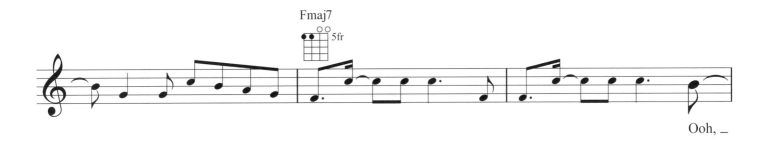

Ooh, _

___ I should be run - nin'.   Ooh, ___ you keep me com - in' ___ for ya.

Speechless

from ALADDIN

Music by Alan Menken
Lyrics by Benj Pasek and Justin Paul

shut me ___ or cut me _____ down. ___ I won't be ___

Chorus

si - lenced. _ You ___ can't keep ___ me qui - et. ____ Won't

trem - ble when _ you try _____ it. All I know ___ is I won't _ go ____

speech - less. _____ 'Cause _ I'll breathe _ when

they try to suf - fo - cate _____ me. ____ Don't you

un - der - es - ti - mate _____ me, 'cause I know _

that I won't go speechless.

Verse

2. Written in stone, ev - 'ry rule, ev - 'ry word, cen - tu - ries old and un - bend - ing.

Stay in your place, bet - ter seen and not heard; well, now that sto - ry is end - ing. 'Cause

Pre-Chorus

I, I can - not start to crum - ble.

So come on and try, ___ try to shut ___ me and cut ___ me ___

down. _____ I won't be ___ si - lenced. _

You can't keep ___ me qui - et. ___ Won't trem - ble when ___ you try ___

___ it. All I know ___ is I won't ___ go ___ speech - less. Speech -

- less. ___ Let the storm in. ___ I can - not ___ be bro -

- ken. ___ No, I won't live ___ un - spo - ken, 'cause I know ___

that I won't go speech - less. _____ Try to ___

Bridge

lock me in ___ this cage, ___ I won't just lay me down _ and die. _

___ I will take these bro - ken wings, _ and watch _ me burn _

___ a - cross _ the sky. ___ Hear the ech - o say - ing I ___

Chorus

___ won't be si - lenced, _____ though

you wan - na see ___ me trem - ble when ___ you try ___

Sucker

Words and Music by Nick Jonas, Joseph Jonas, Miles Ale,
Ryan Tedder, Louis Bell, Adam Feeney and Kevin Jonas

Talk

Words and Music by Khalid Robinson, Guy Lawrence and Howard Lawrence

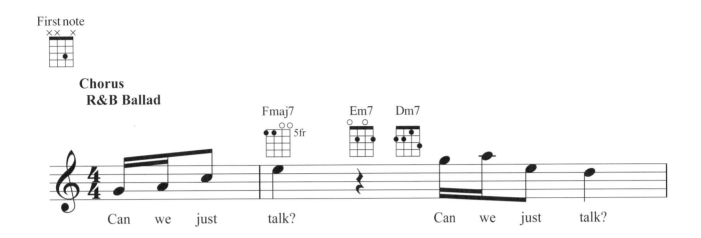

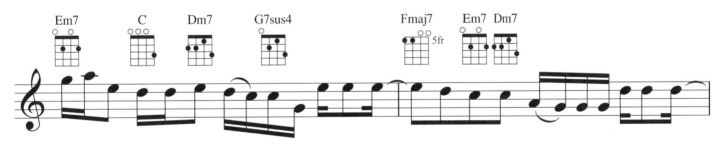

Fig-ure out where we're _ go - ing. Yeah.

Verse

1. Start-ed off ___ right, I can no.
2. Pent - house _ view, left some

see it in your eyes, I can tell ___ that you're want - ing
flow - ers in the room. I'll make sure I leave the door un -

more. What's been on your mind? There's no
locked. Now I'm on the way,

rea - son we should hide. Tell me some - thing I ain't heard be -
swear I won't be late. I'll be there by ___ five o' -

fore. Oh, ___ I've been dream - ing 'bout it ___ and it's you I'm
clock. Oh, ___ you've been dream - ing 'bout it ___ and I'm what you

on.
want. } So stop think - ing 'bout it. ___ Can we just

Sweet but Psycho

**Words and Music by Amanda Koci, Andreas Haukeland,
William Lobban Bean, Henry Walter and Madison Love**

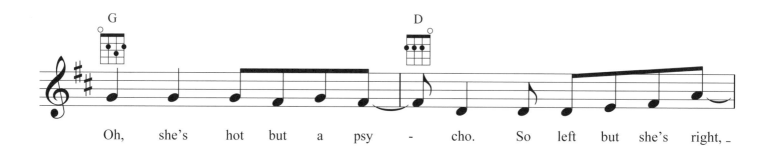

Oh, she's sweet but a psy - cho, a lit - tle bit psy -

- cho. At night she's scream - in', "I'm - ma - ma out ___ my mind." ___

Oh, she's hot but a psy - cho. So left but she's right, ___

___ though. At night she's scream - in', "I'm - ma - ma out ___ my mind." ___

Grab a cop gun, kind - a cra - zy. She's poi - son but tas -

- ty. Yeah, peo - ple say, "Run, don't walk a - way." ___

Walk Me Home

Words and Music by Alecia Moore, Scott Harris and Nate Ruess

know it's get - ting late, so what do you say we leave this

show me how we're good. I think that we could do some

§ Chorus

place? __

good. __

Walk me home __ in the dead of night.

I can't be __ a - lone with all that's on my mind. So,

To Coda ⊕

say you'll stay __ with me to - night. 'Cause there is so much wrong

1. go - ing on __ out - side. 3. There's

2. **Interlude**

Ooh. _____ Ooh. _____

side.

Pre-Chorus

Walk me home __ in the dead of night. 'Cause I can't be __ a - lone with all that's

on my mind. Say you'll stay __ with me to -

D.S. al Coda

night. 'Cause there is so much wrong go - ing on.

Coda

so much wrong, there is so much wrong, there is

so much wrong go - ing on __ out - side.

You Need to Calm Down

Words and Music by Taylor Swift and Joel Little

I ain't tryin' to mess with your self - ex - pres - sion but I've learned the les -
You just need to take sev - 'ral seats and then try to re - store the peace

son that stress - ing and ob - sess - ing 'bout some - bod - y else is no
and con - trol your urg - es to scream a - bout all the peo - ple you

fun.
hate;

And snakes and stones nev - er broke my bones. } So,
'cause shade nev - er made an - y - bod - y less gay. }

Chorus

(Oh, oh, oh, oh, oh, oh, oh, oh.) ____

oh, oh, _____ you need to calm down. _ You're be - ing too

(Oh, oh, oh, oh, oh, oh, oh, oh, ___ oh.)

loud. _ And I'm just like, oh, oh, _____ you need to just

stop. _ Like, can you just not _ step on my gown? You need to calm down.

Ride the Ukulele Wave!

The Beach Boys for Ukulele

This folio features 20 favorites, including: Barbara Ann • Be True to Your School • California Girls • Fun, Fun, Fun • God Only Knows • Good Vibrations • Help Me Rhonda • I Get Around • In My Room • Kokomo • Little Deuce Coupe • Sloop John B • Surfin' U.S.A. • Wouldn't It Be Nice • and more!

00701726 . . . . $14.99

Disney Songs for Ukulele

20 great Disney classics arranged for all uke players, including: Beauty and the Beast • Bibbidi-Bobbidi-Boo (The Magic Song) • Can You Feel the Love Tonight • Chim Chim Cher-ee • Heigh-Ho • It's a Small World • Some Day My Prince Will Come • We're All in This Together • When You Wish upon a Star • and more.

00701708 . . . . $14.99

Jack Johnson – Strum & Sing

Cherry Lane Music
Strum along with 41 Jack Johnson songs using this top-notch collection of chords and lyrics just for the uke! Includes: Better Together • Bubble Toes • Cocoon • Do You Remember • Flake • Fortunate Fool • Good People • Holes to Heaven • Taylor • Tomorrow Morning • and more.

02501702 . . . . $19.99

The Beatles for Ukulele

Ukulele players can strum, sing and pick along with 20 Beatles classics! Includes: All You Need Is Love • Eight Days a Week • Good Day Sunshine • Here, There and Everywhere • Let It Be • Love Me Do • Penny Lane • Yesterday • and more.

00700154 . . . . $16.99

First 50 Songs You Should Play on Ukulele

An amazing collection of 50 accessible, must-know favorites: Edelweiss • Hey, Soul Sister • I Walk the Line • I'm Yours • Imagine • Over the Rainbow • Peaceful Easy Feeling • The Rainbow Connection • Riptide • and many more.

00149250 . . . . $14.99

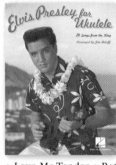

Elvis Presley for Ukulele

arr. Jim Beloff
20 classic hits from The King: All Shook Up • Blue Hawaii • Blue Suede Shoes • Can't Help Falling in Love • Don't • Heartbreak Hotel • Hound Dog • Jailhouse Rock • Love Me • Love Me Tender • Return to Sender • Suspicious Minds • Teddy Bear • and more.

00701004 . . . . $15.99

The Daily Ukulele

compiled and arranged by
Liz and Jim Beloff
Strum a different song everyday with easy arrangements of 365 of your favorite songs in one big songbook! Includes favorites by the Beatles, Beach Boys, and Bob Dylan, folk songs, pop songs, kids' songs, Christmas carols, and Broadway and Hollywood tunes, all with a spiral binding for ease of use.

00240356 . . . . $39.99

Folk Songs for Ukulele

A great collection to take along to the campfire! 60 folk songs, including: Amazing Grace • Buffalo Gals • Camptown Races • For He's a Jolly Good Fellow • Good Night Ladies • Home on the Range • I've Been Working on the Railroad • Kumbaya • My Bonnie Lies over the Ocean • On Top of Old Smoky • Scarborough Fair • Swing Low, Sweet Chariot • Take Me Out to the Ball Game • Yankee Doodle • and more.

00696068 . . . . $12.99

Jake Shimabukuro – Peace Love Ukulele

Deemed "the Hendrix of the ukulele," Hawaii native Jake Shimabukuro is a uke virtuoso. Our songbook features note-for-note transcriptions with ukulele tablature of Jake's masterful playing on all the CD tracks: Bohemian Rhapsody • Boy Meets Girl • Bring Your Adz • Hallelujah • Pianoforte 2010 • Variation on a Dance 2010 • and more, plus two bonus selections!

00702516 . . . . $19.99

The Daily Ukulele – Leap Year Edition

366 More Songs for Better Living
compiled and arranged by
Liz and Jim Beloff
An amazing second volume with 366 MORE songs for you to master each day of a leap year! Includes: Ain't No Sunshine • Calendar Girl • I Got You Babe • Lean on Me • Moondance • and many, many more.

00240681 . . . . $39.99

Hawaiian Songs for Ukulele

Over thirty songs from the state that made the ukulele famous, including: Beyond the Rainbow • Hanalei Moon • Ka-lu-a • Lovely Hula Girl • Mele Kalikimaka • One More Aloha • Sea Breeze • Tiny Bubbles • Waikiki • and more.

00696065 . . . . $10.99

Worship Songs for Ukulele

25 worship songs: Amazing Grace (My Chains are Gone) • Blessed Be Your Name • Enough • God of Wonders • Holy Is the Lord • How Great Is Our God • In Christ Alone • Love the Lord • Mighty to Save • Sing to the King • Step by Step • We Fall Down • and more.

00702546 . . . . $14.99

Disney characters and artwork © Disney Enterprises, Inc.

HAL•LEONARD®

Prices, contents, and availability subject to change.

0119
479